River

River

Poems by

Maryann Hurtt

Kelsay Books

© 2016 Maryann Hurtt. All rights reserved. This material may not be reproduced in any form, published, reprinted, recorded, performed, broadcast, rewritten or redistributed without the explicit permission of Maryann Hurtt. All such actions are strictly prohibited by law.

Cover design: Jim Hurtt
Cover photograph: Corey J. Hurtt

ISBN 13: 978-1-945752-11-7

Kelsay Books
Aldrich Press
www.kelsaybooks.com

With appreciation and deep gratitude to my fellow
poets, family, creatures, friends, and mentors.
Thank you, all of you, kin.

Acknowledgments

Grateful acknowledgement is made to the publications in which the following poems first appeared, sometimes in previous versions or with different titles.

Ariel: "Astrophysics"
Cancer Poetry Project 2: "Hired Man Down"
Stoneboat: "Picking Blackberries With My Mother, Fifty Years Ago"
Verse & Vision: "Dreaming Snowy Egret"
Verse Wisconsin: "The Old Men"
Wisconsin People & Ideas: "Ground Cherries"
Wisconsin Poets' Calendar: "May Day," "Sinew and Sweat"
YourDailyPoem: "For the Love of Pisces"

Contents

For the Love of Pisces	13
Molting Season	14
Trinity	15
May Day	16
Waiting	17
Picking Blackberries with My Mother, Fifty Years Ago	18
Killing Field	19
Astrophysics	20
Her Not So Final Resting Place	21
Sinew and Sweat	22
Father the Reverend Adelir Antonio Di Carli	23
A Poet's Possibly More Glorious Death	24
Hour of Divine Mercy	25
Hired Man Down	26
Uncommon Substance	27
Father Bird	28
Ground Cherries	29
One More Day	30
Dreaming Snowy Egret	31
The Trapeze Artist	32
Snail Time	33
The Old Men	34
Plainsong	35
Cadence	36
River	37

About the Author

Eventually all things merge into one,
and a river runs through it.

—Norman Maclean

For the Love of Pisces

on this maybe
spring day
sun with different slant
tentative green willows
most everything still gray
I see a young boy
pumping against the wind
he carries a fish in one hand
its tail flipping the road
with every revolution
of the bike wheel
leaving the marsh
where a bit ago
the fish knew home

I wonder how fast
life changes
how our lives
so depend on someone else's
how we come to know
each other
in so many ways
dead or alive

Molting Season

you teeter on fragile legs
pull chemo tufts of hair
fling them out the back door

your once muscled body
now shrunk
welcomes new air
then retreats back in

today you make comfort
for sparrows
you will never know

they find shelter
in dwellings created
by hair
no longer yours

hope breathes
in tangled nests and rhythms

you bless tomorrow

Trinity

I sit shivering
in my father's drift boat
the sun has not found its way
over the Cascades
the man I spent my first eighteen years
waits next to me
he's 92 now
still rises when it's dark
loves these invisible salmon
like brothers
my husband pushes-pulls oars
through mountain cold McKenzie water
we cast lines
ponder fish journeys
to eat what has worked so hard
feels like communion
the river, my prayer

May Day

on May day
when cowslips and skunk cabbage
crawl their way up
these marshy woods
a great blue heron
laces through tangled trees
to LaBudde creek
where tiny fish begin
their journey
learn to swim
and sometimes fly
in the long throat
of a prehistoric bird
whose wings dance
with tamaracks
so that even death
is grace

Waiting

I wait for your breaths
count their ups and downs
chickadees out the south window
do their suet dance
the cats hover
your almost still body
back porch
tiny end of season roses
hold teaspoons of snow
the 3:10 freight screeches
two long, one short, one long
you wait at the crossing
daring to leap

Picking Blackberries with My Mother, Fifty Years Ago

my blackberry fingers
lick my mother's hand
her voice whispers
between
a rock
and the hard place
of tiny graves

she holds fast
my fist
that I might stay
on this side of the cliff,
not lost in clouds,
or wherever
my baby brother
slipped away

Killing Field

once again
I go to the killing field
and like every spring
find bleached raccoon skulls
lying among purple anemone
their eyeless sockets
stare into a sky
so blue
it almost blinds me
into seeing

I want to know
their lives, their deaths
how beneath my feet
crumpled leaves
will soon be dirt
how it's possible
to come up purple blossom
and how to the east
sandhill cranes honk their dinosaur songs
even as we slide from breath
to breathless
and breath all over again

Astrophysics

on this loony tune
full moon
of a morning

you got up
and left

moon's luminescence
gave you courage
to break tethers
held way too long

dying really isn't so difficult
when you understand
cosmic flight

no simple angel wings for you
your compass sent you
soaring
finally dancing
stardust

the universe
ready to give birth to you
over and over again

Her Not So Final Resting Place

my mother sits in the bedroom closet
going on five years now
amazing how she still hollers
even with all that dust
in her mouth
You're wearing that?!
Don't eat that junk!
You're late! Wake up!
one of these days
my brother and I will get her
to Arlington
where our left way-too-early sibling
waits patiently
but in the meantime
she is content
to bark out instructions
with an occasional
I still love you

Sinew and Sweat

the fox comes out a hole
his tail a comet
in early light

in dew damp woods
we run together
no longer fox or human
simply sinew and sweat

earth's lub-dub
oaks, moraines, and the tiny rodent
he had for breakfast

Father the Reverend Adelir Antonio Di Carli

bound to party balloons
Father the Reverend Adelir Antonio Di Carli
lifted off Paranagua on Sunday
soon a speck in the universe
and never heard from again

sky so deep
oceans so high
infinity has no limits
when we let go earthly fetters

do you think he knew that day
he'd be riding in a great white's belly
or maybe an albatross's beak?

a view so unexpected
he thought he had discovered
a new heaven

A Poet's Possibly More Glorious Death

days before she died
her heart losing rhythm and muscle
the bookshelf above her bed
packed with a lifetime of journeys
crashed

the weight of words, ideas, paper, glue

she wondered at the possibilities
had she been lying in bed
that particular moment

what a smashing way to exit
what a crescendo

Hour of Divine Mercy

the nurse wakes at dawn
startling deep sleep for the page
to tell her
someone has grown wings
in these wee hours
of divine mercy
she has read the explanations
how the heart
at this hour
goes rogue and all rhythm is lost
but she knows better
how when on a journey
of such monumental importance
it is good to leave early
catch the sunrise
even when clouds roll in and roll back
confounding
those left behind

Hired Man Down

the hired man
lies in musty sheets and patched quilts
his room partitioned
from the barn
stacks of National Geographic
piled neatly in the corner
dry hay, greasy tools,
and manure insulate
against early spring chill

his one window
leaks the farm kids' giggles
they tiptoe into his room
rock back and forth
with questions
about the old man
they never knew to be down

his breaths get noisy
his gut draining away
the air around him
fills with odor
so different than the sweet smell of manure

he knows what he has to do
lie low, breathe in, breathe out
slower and slower

the animals taught him well
this is, after all, no tragedy
but what we all must do some day
this man just more intimate
with the seasons
the rest of us still fear

Uncommon Substance

his eyes watch over the old nurse
in his time-stuck
World War II picture
she lies in bed
oxygen tubing now her companion
memories, too
Sicily, France, Africa
the blood of soldiers
forever blended
in her shrinking body
she says she has no regrets
this life of uncommon substance
where the smell of roses
shares equal time with metallic reek
of warm blood
she has known it all
soon she won't be fighting
for another breath
what escapes now
will join the exhalations
of what we give back
when we're done here

Father Bird

> "The battles of the Eastern Front (World War II) constituted the largest military confrontation in history . . ."
> —*The Atlantic*

maybe there really is a heaven
and we'll all meet again

the emaciated Russian woman
will greet him
with memory of a German officer
feeding mush
into her infant's wailing mouth

the child lived
she died
he survived

now hours before his death
he wonders his life

can one kindness
clean the rot of war?

can the life-death
multiplication, subtraction, addition, division
balance the horror
still inside

Will she know him?

Ground Cherries

I sit at her table
and eat ground cherries
she peels their lantern paper skin
makes little stacks of pale orange balls

She's almost ninety years old
her skin is translucent
like the tiny fruits
she carefully opens for me

If I listen long enough
I will know what nourishment
has held her up so long
and makes her rise every morning

I will learn
how much deeper
we need to go
to find succulent fruit
in what we assume so frail

One More Day

in the last month
of the last year
of her eighty- plus- five year life
she found gravity
was no longer her friend
pulled by some diabolical force
she found herself
on the bathroom floor
how she longed
for sweet decaying bark, fern fronds
and sturdy feet
to deliver her away

she knows soon she will break free
of all gravity laws
but now
all she wishes
is one more blue sky day
a mind clear enough
to hear ever green songs
and to love this earth
enough
to fly

Dreaming Snowy Egret

in an ocean
of marshy grass
mallards, teals, pintails
flutter in a confusion
of color

a single snowy egret
stands
stone still
regal and almost blinding
white

I want to learn
the music of silence
know water
as friend
my heart beat
a benign clock

The Trapeze Artist

I know a man
who when trying to die
hung on to a carcass
way too long
when young that body
never betrayed him
circus days
women galore
speedy cars
a life at least some would covet
but now his days are long
each breath a conscious
in and out
harder and harder
till at last
his arms begin to beat
up and out
breaths longer and longer between
till at last invisible wings
swing low, sweet chariot

Snail Time

the snail on my parents'
front walk
paces its slow but sometime
will get there crawl to the azalea bush
leaves just a trace
of coming and going
his shell both shelter
and what seems to be baggage
too heavy to carry

my mother lies in the hospice bed
it almost swallows her
my father marks a trail between
the kitchen and her bed
carries warmed coffee
tiny comfort in a long day

I ask my father about
the snail
the heavy shell
the long slow crawl
you do what you have to do

The Old Men

at the pow wow
tap dirt
that has held them
for how long
they draw circles
hear fossil rhythms

soon the dirt
will let them go
then scudding leaves
free falling clouds
maybe the beating
of fox arteries

in the end
we become
what we love

the rain starts to fall
it's so much easier to travel
as vapor

Plainsong

every day now
the doe sinks deeper
and deeper
her ribs out of the snow
like dense harp strings
the bass notes
deep
like the plainsong
I want to chant
and remember how once
she traced the woods
with valentine hoof prints
her essence
still blessing us

Cadence

the old nurse lies awake
counts heart beats
hers and all the other lub-dubs
listened to
and now tallied after so many years
she remembers the wonder
of first heart beats
last heart beats
how even with silence
she knows the rhythm carries on
sweet sting consolation
for the quiet
she understands is coming

River

with its polished stones
and cold, cold water
almost metallic taste
calls me home
carrying crawdads and algae
larvae of creatures ready
to make new life
then food
for someone else
we float on journeys
we are never sure of
bounce from shore to currents
to near drowning
finally learn the buoyancy of something
holding us
in watery arms
where we departed
where we return

About the Author

After almost thirty years working as a hospice nurse, Maryann Hurtt is now retired and lives down the road from the Ice Age Trail in Wisconsin. The stories she witnessed all those years and the natural world around her profoundly influence her writing and life. She has co-facilitated a "Language of Nature" program at her community's environmental park for six years and has participated in several art-poetry projects. Her poetry has been published online in *Portage, Your Daily Poem, Blue Heron,* a variety of journals including *Verse Wisconsin, Stoneboat, Fox Cry Review, Wisconsin People & Ideas,* and a few anthologies. She co-authored, with Cynthia Frozena, a hospice care planning book. The Wisconsin Fellowship of Poets, The Cancer Poetry Project, The Wisconsin Academy of Arts and Sciences, and The Oncology Nursing Society have awarded her writing and she has received scholarships from the Prague Summer Program, Fishtrap, and Bread Loaf-Orion.

Made in the USA
Middletown, DE
24 October 2022